THE PRESBYTERIAN TRUSTEE

Other books by Earl S. Johnson, Jr., published by Geneva Press

Selected to Serve: A Guide for Church Officers
The Presbyterian Deacon: An Essential Guide
Witness without Parallel: Eight Biblical Texts That Make Us
 Presbyterian

THE PRESBYTERIAN TRUSTEE

AN ESSENTIAL GUIDE

Earl S. Johnson, Jr.

Geneva Press
Louisville, Kentucky

Book design by Sharon Adams
Cover design by Night & Day Design

First edition
Published by Geneva Press
Louisville, Kentucky

This book is printed on acid-free paper that meets the American National Standards Institute Z39.48 standard. ∞

PRINTED IN THE UNITED STATES OF AMERICA

04 05 06 07 08 09 10 11 12 13 — 10 9 8 7 6 5 4 3 2 1

Library of Congress Cataloging-in-Publication Data

Johnson, Earl S., 1942-
    The Presbyterian trustee : an essential guide / Earl S. Johnson, Jr. — 1st ed.
        p. cm.
    Includes bibliographical references (p.).
    ISBN 0-664-50255-5 (alk. paper)
    1. Church trustees.   2. Presbyterian Church (U.S.A.)—Government.   3. Presbyterian Church—Government.   I. Title.

BX9195.J633 2004
254'.051—dc22

2003064222

Contents

Introduction

Although a number of manuals and guides exist to help train officers in general, and elders and deacons in particular,[1] nothing extensive has been written for trustees in the Presbyterian church since 1939, when John Murdock MacInnis published *The Trustee and the Church Today: A Study in the Christian Way of Doing Business.*

Why is such a book needed now? One answer is that all Presbyterian churches, regardless of the organization of church boards they adopt, are required by our *Constitution* to have trustees (G-7.0401).

Congregations that function with bicameral boards (with a separate session and a board of trustees) need to be sure that trustees are not ignored in officer training or treated like stepchildren in the collegium of officers. Too often their role is considered to be secondary because they are not ordained officers or because it is thought that their work is primarily "practical" rather than "spiritual." The *Constitution* makes it clear, however, that trustees are given important responsibilities to fulfill and that proper preparation is as necessary for them as it is for ministers, elders, or deacons. Guidelines and training materials are needed to assist them as they carry out critical administrative, financial, maintenance, construction, and personnel functions.

Even if congregations do not have a separate board, they still are required to have trustees to fulfill state laws of incorporation. Financial and administrative responsibilities must be carried out by the elders on the session (in a unicameral board structure) or by the deacons who are assigned the trustees' functions. As the *Book of Order* puts it,

> The elders in active service in a church who are eligible under the civil law shall, by reason of their office, be the trustees of such corporation, unless the corporation shall determine another method for electing its trustees. (G-7.0401)

> Deacons may be appointed by governing bodies to serve on committees or as trustees. (G-6.0406)

(It should be recognized at the start that the duties of trustees developed very differently in the history of the northern [UPCUSA] and southern [PCUS] branches of the church. In many former PCUS congregations, trustees act mainly as legal agents to implement session decisions about real estate. Church officers and pastors in those churches need to realize that what is written in this book will be especially useful for elders and/or deacons, since they assume the responsibilities in the southern church stream that is taken on by the trustees in other parts of the country.)

A book for trustees serves one other purpose. The demands on administrators and financial officers are so intense in contemporary society, fund-raising is so challenging, building and fire codes are so stringent, costs escalate at such exponential rates, accounting requires such rigorous honesty and accuracy (especially in light of corporate scandals revealed at the beginning of the twenty-first century), wise investment of ecclesiastical funds demands so much good judgment, and personnel matters are so time-consuming that the church needs to provide fundamental background information to lighten the load of those who are asked to engage in work that is critical for the future life of the local church and the whole denomination.

This book uses a general approach that is designed to be helpful to all congregations. For every church, regardless of size or location, the fundamentals are the same, as are the biblical models for the work of trustees, the historic background, the responsibilities (spiritual and secular), the principles of financial management and professional integrity, and the challenges that the future may bring. Beyond the universal issues that apply to the functions of trustees, each church needs to work with business administrators, attorneys, or the local presbytery to develop guidelines that will be useful in its particular locale.

My own work with trustees has been carried on for more than thirty-five years, in six different churches, during which time I have served as an associate pastor, senior pastor, or stated supply. My heartfelt thanks is extended to men and women in churches of various sizes, from twelve members to more than fourteen hundred members, in Idaho (Twin Falls) and New York (West Charlton, West Galway, Plattsburgh, Pittsford, and Johnstown), who taught me just how important the administrative work of the church really is and how God leads those who are entrusted with it in Christ's name.

Let me also express gratitude to three people who read a preliminary version of the book and made numerous suggestions and offered corrections that improved its quality and accuracy. Thanks go to Chandlee Gill, stated clerk of the Presbytery of Albany; Eric Graninger, general counsel, Legal Services/Risk Management, PC(USA); and W. Taylor Reveley III, dean and professor of law, William and Mary Law School (and a Presbyterian trustee). My appreciation also needs to be expressed to Robert Bullock, retired editor of *Presbyterian Outlook*, who gave permission to reprint materials already published. I am also grateful to David Dobson, senior editor at Geneva Press, for guiding me graciously through the whole writing and editing process, and to Daniel Braden, associate managing editor, for his perceptive advice during the final stages.

Chapter 1

Biblical Models

Although the office of trustee cannot be traced directly to ancient biblical roots, as the roles of pastor, elder, and deacon can, since it is one that was established within the past three hundred years (see the discussion in chapter 2 below), the fundamental duties of that office are clearly outlined in central scriptural texts.

Why are these models important? By ignoring the biblical foundation of church administration we have often misunderstood the work of trustees. From one perspective it has been undervalued, by considering it to be one merely of practicality, in contrast to the responsibilities of the session or the board of deacons, which are defined to be more ecclesiastical and spiritual. "Leave the running of the church to the trustees," members often say, "but let the elders and deacons do the worship planning, praying, recruiting of new members, and pastoral care." Ironically, just the opposite attitude can prevail. In some churches members think that trustees really manage the church, since they make all the important decisions and the other officers deal only with "spiritual" matters.

Such a bifurcation of responsibilities among church officers creates an unnecessary and misleading distinction. Administration involves more than the practical direction of the church, important as that is. It is also a gift of the Holy Spirit. Even though the office of trustee is a relatively new one, the work of administration is blessed by God and is dependent upon God's call and the power of the Spirit.

1 Corinthians 12: Administration as a Spiritual Gift

The importance of the gifts of administration is especially spelled out in 1 Corinthians 12, a seminal chapter that describes the various roles of called workers in the church. Paul indicates carefully that although there are varieties of gifts, there is but one Spirit. Even though these gifts (called *charismata* in Greek) are very different, "All these are activated by one and the same Spirit, who allots to each one individually just as the Spirit chooses" (12:11).

Administrative gifts are mentioned not once but twice at the end of chapter 12 (vv. 27–28). In the NRSV they are translated "forms of assistance" and "forms of leadership" and are valued equally with all the others.

Now you are the body of Christ and individually members of it. And God has appointed in the church first apostles, second prophets, third teachers; then deeds of power, then gifts of healing, *forms of assistance*, *forms of leadership,* various kinds of tongues. (emphasis added)

Some biblical interpreters contend that the administrative gifts are secondary because they require only technical skills or because they are inferior to the primary callings of apostles, prophets, and teachers, which appear to be in order of significance. But such thinking is misleading. The preceding verses in chapter 12 make it clear that the one body of Christ does not have any superior or inferior parts. Even the "weaker" or "less honorable" parts are given special respect so that the body can function effectively and in a united manner. What is more, it would be an inexcusable sign of pride for any member to think that he or she is so important that it is unnecessary to belong to the body. It would be a ridiculous sight to find a congregation that consisted only of an enormous mouth in the pulpit or a grotesque foot lumbering down the church aisle all by itself on Sunday morning.

Paul insists that we are in it together and that we all need each other. The body of Christ, after all, is Christ's body, not ours. Jesus Christ is the head of the body and even though some functions might appear to us at times to be more important than others, to God they are all part of the whole.

The unity may be the most recognizable when there is a crisis. If the body has a toothache or a paper cut on the finger, we do not say simply, "My tooth hurts," but "I do not feel well," meaning that the whole self is sick. As Paul puts it, "If one member suffers, all suffer together with it; if one member is honored, all rejoice together with it" (v. 26). If the finances of the church are in disarray, we know that it is not just bill paying that is in trouble; all the programs of the church are jeopardized.

Obviously not all members of the church have identical spiritual gifts and personal talents; all cannot do the same things at once.

> Are all apostles? Are all prophets? Are all teachers? Do all work miracles? Do all possess gifts of healing? Do all speak in tongues? Do all interpret? But strive for the greater gifts. (vv. 29–31)

Nevertheless, Paul makes it clear that differences do not create spiritual hierarchy. The only superiority in the church is that of "the greater gifts" (v. 31), the highest being the love mentioned in chapter 13, and love is not something that only apostles, prophets, and teachers can expect to receive. It is the hope for all members of Christian congregations, and all church workers and volunteers, especially those who have been given gifts of the Spirit to be used for the work of the body. The session is the ruling body of the church and has final decision-making power, but this fact does not mean that the responsibilities of the elders are more important than those of other members of the church who are under the session's authority and direction.

What is the nature of the gifts that apply directly to the work of the trustees? Unfortunately the expressions "forms of assistance" and "forms of leadership," which are used to translate Paul's words in 1 Corinthians 12:28 in the NRSV, are somewhat vague and lose the power and the dynamic significance of the original Greek. The word for "forms of assistance" (*antilēmpsis*), for example, literally means "helping" or "protecting," and the text could be translated "acts of enabling," "acts of administration," or "administrative work." A recent biblical commentator thinks that it refers to support staff and indicates that those who help others in the church to do their jobs well clearly have a God-given talent. Good management skills come from the Holy Spirit and are certainly as important as the more conspicuous or spontaneous charismata like preaching or speaking in tongues.[1]

The second descriptor, "forms of leadership" (*kybernēsis*), literally means "administration." In a related form (*kybernētēs*) it refers to a "master," "pilot," or "helmsman" of a sailing vessel. In ancient Greek literature the pilot was the one who knew the times of the day and the year, the sky, the stars, the currents, and where the sandbars were in various ports.[2] In the Greek version of the Old Testament (Septuagint) it refers to a person who has God's wisdom and knows how to listen to others, gain in learning, and acquire discerning skill (Prov. 1:5). The *kybernētēs* is one who can provide upright guidance to the king: ". . . in an abundance of counselors there is safety" (cf. 24:6).[3]

Paul, as a seasoned traveler, one who had experienced storms and shipwrecks at sea himself (2 Cor. 11:25; Acts 27), may well have had this image of the administrator as the one who steers in rough water or the critical leader in times of trouble in mind. As Hermann Beyer puts it, "The reference can only be to the specific gifts which qualify a Christian to be a helmsman to his [*sic*] congregation, i.e., a true director of its order and therewith of its life. . . . The importance of the helmsman increases in a time of storm. The office of directing the congregation may well have developed especially in emergencies both within and without."[4]

For Paul, the administrator is an officer who is critical for the safe passage of the ship of the church, but it must also be pointed out that the pilot or the one at the helm is not the owner of the ship or the captain. He or she does not even set the course or determine the cargo but is responsible for guiding the ship out of the harbor to a place where it can sail to predetermined destinations.

Such an image provides a good model for understanding the role of the trustee in the Presbyterian church today. Although the work of the trustees is critical for the proper functioning of the church, as administrators they do not make policy decisions for the congregation but take orders from the captain, Jesus Christ, the head of the body. They also receive necessary direction from the session, which is the ruling body of the church as it provides "support . . . review, and control" (G-10.0102m). No wonder that one commentator translates Paul's description of the work of the church administrator as the "ability to formulate strategies."[5]

The Administrator as Treasurer, Manager, Trustee, and Steward

In other biblical passages additional models for administrative service are borrowed from government and business practices common in the ancient world. Titles like treasurer, manager, and steward point to the connection between business administration and spiritual leadership and demonstrate how God uses officers with financial skills and administrative authority to serve divine purposes. They also indicate the high expectation that the church had of its first administrative teams.

In the Old Testament, for example, when the Jewish people were freed from exile and the time came for the restoration of the Jerusalem temple, King Cyrus of Persia organized the administration of the whole venture (Ezra 1:8) through the agency of the imperial treasurer (*gizbar*). Later, King Artaxerxes ordered all the regional treasurers in the area called "Beyond the River" to cooperate fully with the Ezra, the scribe of the law of heaven, and reminded them of their primary accountability to God. Whatever the priest required of them had to be done with all diligence (Ezra 7:21). "Whatever is commanded by the God of heaven, let it be done for the zeal of the house of heaven" (Ezra 7:23; cf. Neh. 13:13; Dan. 3:2–3). To Ezra it was a sign of God's blessing and steadfast love that the king and all the members of his administration were commanded to glorify the house of the Lord (8:28–29).

In the New Testament Paul indicates that financial officers were also held in high regard in the early church when he includes Erastus, a city treasurer (*oikonomos*), among those who send greetings with him to the believers in Rome (Rom. 16:23). The position of "steward of the city" or chamberlain was one of responsibility in the ancient world, often held by slaves or freed slaves (a class from which many of the first Christians came), and it is possible that Erastus is the same Roman aedile whose name has been discovered by archaeologists in an inscription listing him as the donor of a paved city block in the city of Corinth about the same time Paul wrote Romans.[6] An aedile was usually elected for one year and was responsible for the maintenance and repair of public roads and buildings, in charge of weights and measures in the markets and the administration of the public games.[7]

When the title *oikonomos* appears in another texts, it is variously translated "trustee," "manager," or "steward" and is the basis of our word *stewardship*. The high standards set for financial officers, the demand that they have a public responsibility to do more than enrich themselves, is indicated in Jesus' parable of the faithful and unfaithful stewards (Luke 12:41–48; Matt. 24:45–51), the story of an estate executive who was expected to be a "faithful and prudent manager" (Luke 12:42). In Luke 16:1–13 Jesus tells a second story about a steward who was squandering the owner's property. This foreman is called to account in a summary fashion when his dishonesty is discovered. "'What is this that I hear about you? Give me an accounting of your management, because you cannot be my manager any longer'" (v. 2). Jesus uses the parable to teach us that all believers, especially those with responsibility, will be held accountable in all things (vv. 10–13):

> Whoever is faithful in a very little is faithful also in much; and whoever is dishonest in a very little is dishonest also in much. If then you have not been faithful with the dishonest wealth [*mammon* in Greek], who will entrust to you the true riches? And if you have not been faithful with what belongs to another, who will give you what is your own?

In 1 Corinthians 4:1–2 Paul similarly uses the title *oikonomos* to indicate the high standards expected of Christian leaders. Those who are called as servants of Christ are stewards of God's mysteries, and they must be found trustworthy. The same term is used to describe the ethical responsibilities of a bishop in the church (Titus 1:7–9): as God's steward he must be blameless, hospitable, a lover of goodness, prudent, upright, devout, and self-controlled. In summary, 1 Peter 4:10 reminds administrators that they must use their gifts for the good of the church and that they are derived only from God: "Like good stewards [*oikonomoi*] of the manifold grace of God, serve one another with whatever gift each of you has received."

Other texts point to the same conclusion. Jesus' actions indicated that he had very little patience with those who mismanaged the money of others or defrauded religious institutions. His harshest criticism was leveled at the temple money changers who had turned the house of God into a den of thieves (Mark 11:15–19 and parallels). The advice in 1 Timothy 3:3, 8 admonishes Christian leaders and administrators not to be greedy for money, that theirs are positions of honesty and integrity. No wonder that the *Book of Order* (G-6.0101) tells church officers first of all that their primary responsibility is to follow the example of Jesus Christ.

> All ministry in the Church is a gift from Jesus Christ. Members and officers alike serve mutually under the mandate of Christ who is the chief minister of all. His ministry is the basis of all ministries; the standard for all offices is the pattern of the one who came "not to be served but to serve." (Matt. 20:28)

Questions for Study

1. Are trustees considered spiritual leaders in your congregation? Are they responsible for any aspects of the mission of the church? Are they included in weekly prayers for church leaders?

2. Take a look at Jesus' parables about managers in Luke 12:41–48 and Luke 16:1–13. What else can you learn about administration and good management from them?

3. Why do you think Jesus and the biblical writers mentioned money and property so often? What should our attitude be as church officers? See Proverbs 1:8–19; 3:5–18; 8:6–21; Matthew 5:3, 21–26; 6:11–12, 25–34; 13:44–45; 19:16–30 and parallels; 20:1–16; 2 Corinthians 8:1–15 for some examples.

Chapter 2

Historical Background

*T*he historic roots of the ministry and duties of contemporary trustees are found in the Reformed principles of civil
and ecclesiastical government and in the American con-
cepts of the separation of church and state developed later
in the colonial and Revolutionary War periods.

Calvin's Perspective of Administrative Offices

The writings of John Calvin and the practice of government
in Geneva profoundly influenced the Presbyterian church's
developing understanding of the relationship between secular and religious powers, and it still impacts our polity and
mission today. Calvin's models were not based entirely on
sixteenth-century business practices but were also informed
by the Reformed principle that all administrative power
comes from God and that all civil, financial, and spiritual
authority is derived from one source.

In Calvin's view there had to be a close relationship between civil and ecclesiastical governments. As outlined in his *Institutes of the Christian Religion* (especially 4.20), civil government had responsibilities to religious bodies to ensure that

- idolatry and sacrilege against God are prevented;
- public tranquility is not disturbed;
- every person is allowed to enjoy his or her property without molestation;
- business is transacted without fraud or injustice;
- integrity and modesty are cultivated.

Nevertheless, Calvin was clear that "human polity" could not be put in charge of the maintenance of religion. Although he approved of civil government that was faithful to true religion found in the law of God, secular authorities could not be allowed to make laws respecting religion and the worship of God.

For Calvin there were three aspects of civil government:

- the magistrate, who was the guardian and conservator of the laws
- the laws according to which the magistrate governs
- the people who are governed and obey

In his view magistrates are more than appointed or elected officials. They have a mandate from God (4.20.4) and must be faithful as God's deputies (4.20.6). "To sum up, if they remember that they are vicars of God, they watch with all care, earnestness, and diligence, to represent in themselves . . . some image of divine providence, protection, goodness, benevolence, and justice" (4.20.6). They should remember that they are occupied not with profane affairs or those alien to a servant of God, but with a most holy office. Thus they should pay attention to both tables of the law, to make sure that love of God and love of neighbor are both respected" (4.20.9). "We see, therefore, that they are ordained protectors and vindicators of public innocence, modesty, decency, and tranquility, and that their sole endeavor should be to provide for the public safety and peace of all" (4.20.9).

In sixteenth-century Geneva the close relationship between civil and ecclesiastical government was exercised in practice as the city was given the responsibility to regulate business for efficiency and justice.[1] The state was to manage weights and measures, interest rates, currency, contracts, public education, health care, and labor relations for the protection of the citizens.

Calvin's principles are particularly evident in regard to the management of the city's hospital in which scattered charitable causes were organized into a kind of United Way overseen by civil authorities. The officers who administered the distribution of the funds were selected from a group of important citizens in the city. As Elsie Ann McKee describes

the arrangement, "Reordering welfare to make it more efficient meant not only centralized funds and better trained
businessmen to administer the money, but also a more ratio-
nal organization of the details of charitable activity."[2] As
she points out, although the use of lay leaders rather than
priests to regulate church activities was not entirely new,
the Reformed emphasis on the priesthood of all believers
provided a new justification for it. In Geneva public and
ecclesiastical funds were combined as both institutions
were made responsible for the public welfare and the care
of the poor.[3]

Trustees and the Constitutional Debate
about Disestablishment

In colonial America the outline of modern trustee functions
began to take clearer shape as lay leaders assumed increas-
ing responsibility for the administrative and financial management of the church. In the early days of settlement there
was no consistency about church-state relationships, since
it differed with the national origin of the settlers in the local
areas.[4] Many colonists came to America in search of religious liberty and with the desire to preserve their own tra-
ditions. In Virginia and the New England colonies practice
was influenced by the Anglican or Congregational model,
in which churches had to be registered with the government
regardless of denominational affiliation, and taxes were

used to support ecclesiastical expenses. In the Middle Atlantic colonies many churches did not adhere to the establishment policies of their brothers and sisters in New England and Virginia. In most areas they did not favor government support of ministry, and in Pennsylvania and Delaware in particular, principles of total religious freedom were strongly espoused. In the Carolinas and Georgia, freedom of worship was also generally supported, and citizens tended to agree that the government's role was to make sure that citizens could practice religion freely without interference, particularly without the levying of taxes to promote religious practice.

In the pre–Revolutionary War period the debate between establishment (government controlled and supported) and disestablishment (free of government influence and support) churches had already begun in earnest. "Religious minorities, especially Baptists, Presbyterians, and Methodists, aggressively fought against the general assessment proposal and were supported by the less religiously orthodox Thomas Jefferson and James Madison."[5] Already in 1752 the Synod of New York argued that churches should be able to raise their own money and control its distribution through elected trustees:

> [I]t is not inconsistent with the presbyterian Plan of Government, or the Institution of our Lord Jesus Christ, that Trustees nor a Committee chosen by the Congregation Should have the Disposal & Application of the publick

> Money raised by sd Congregation, to the Uses for which
> it was designed: provided that they leave in the Hands &
> to the Management of the Deacons, what is collected for
> the Lords Table & the Poor. And That Ministers of the
> Gospel by virtue of their Office have no right to Sit with
> or preside over such Trustees or Committees.[6]

In the period from 1776 to 1786 when most of the thir-
teen original states were writing their constitutions, the
concept of disestablishment gained ascendancy. When
churches that had been receiving money from local governments were given the freedom to raise and spend their
own funds, they were also required by most states to incor-
porate and elect trustees who were responsible for the management of financial assets, whether they were received by
voluntary donation or general assessment. Trustees were
elected or appointed to raise, hold, and disperse monies; in
1788, when the first Presbyterian constitution was written,
they were charged to take care of "temporal concerns." In
1799 the General Assembly declared and constituted "a corporation and body politic corporate, in law and in fact, to
have continuance forever by the name, style and title of
'Trustees of the General Assembly of the Presbyterian
Church in the United States of America.'" Said trustees
were to be "persons able and capable in law as well as to
take, receive and hold, all and all manner of lands, tene-
ments, rents, annuities, franchises and other hereditaments,
which at any time or times heretofore have been granted,

bargained, sold, enfeoffed, released, devised, or otherwise conveyed"[7] to the church. The trustees were also to have authority to dispose of church property, could sue and be sued, and could do anything that any other person, or bodies politic or corporate, was legally able to do. By 1833 all state constitutions had adopted the disestablishment principle, and religious organizations were free of a direct connection to any state government.[8]

These actions were part, of course, of the larger debate that occupied the states, the Continental Congress, and the Constitutional Convention, during and after the Revolutionary War, concerning religious liberty and the establishment of religion. Seminal documents included James Madison's *A Memorial and Remonstrance Against Religious Assessments* (1785) and Thomas Jefferson's *Bill for Establishing a Provision for Teachers of the Christian Religion* (1784) and *Bill for Religious Liberty* (1785), all of which influenced the writing and adoption of the First Amendment. The so-called establishment clause, listed first in the Bill of Rights, prohibits Congress from setting up any religion as a state religion or preventing the free exercise of any religion:

> Congress shall make no law respecting an establishment of religion, or prohibiting the free exercise thereof; or abridging the freedom of speech, or the right of the people peaceably to assemble, and to petition the Government for a redress of grievances.

The exact meaning of the First Amendment (its "original intent") was controversial from the beginning and is still debated today. Generally speaking, the *separationist* or *broad* interpretation favors a strict separation of church and state, whereas the *accommodationist* or *nonpreferential* point of view contends that the amendment was intended merely to prevent one religion, sect, or denomination from having a position of national power, not to prohibit the government from giving aid to religious organizations. Separationists argue that the government cannot restrict religious expression in any way unless it is dangerous to individual health or trespasses against public law. The accommodationist view contends that state and local laws can regulate religions as long as they do not discriminate against particular religious organizations.

Trustees and other church leaders can easily recognize the importance of the ongoing debate about these definitions in the twenty-first century, since the conclusions one reaches impact the answers given to contemporary questions about the proper ownership of church property, religious demonstrations against the government, the teaching of evolution in public schools, and the use of state and federal funds for charitable or religious work.

Development and Modification

In the years that followed the passage of the Constitution and the approval of the Bill of Rights, the duties of trustees in religious bodies took on various aspects. Some of them still pertain in churches today, while others have been changed or have fallen away. Although laws respecting the corporate nature of religious institutions vary from state to state, a number of general principles were established, often through the rulings of state and federal courts:[9]

- In order for members to vote at an election held by a corporate religious society, individuals often had to attend divine worship and contribute financially to the support of the church. In the PC(USA) only active members may vote for the election of officers (G-5.0202; 7.0301).
- In many churches trustees did not necessarily have to be members of the church they represented; often they were leading businessmen who had no direct connection with the congregation. Later it was decided that at least two-thirds of the board had to be members of the individual church. In the PC(USA) only members on the active roll of the church may be elected as trustees (G-7.0401).
- Trustees, deacons, wardens, and similar officers were ordered by the courts to be given the same power as officers of other incorporated societies to manage, use, and employ gifts and grants made to these bodies.
- The legal title to property was vested in the trustees of the church, but they could not pervert the purpose of the trust. Their power was subordinate to the customs and laws of the organization (G-8.0201).

- Trustees could approve contracts for a church but were not permitted to buy or sell property without the approval of the congregation (G-7.0402; 7.0304a[4]; 8.0501). They could act only for the benefit of the congregation as a whole and could not bind the society beyond the powers granted to them. Acts of individual trustees were illegal unless authorized by the whole board at a stated or special meeting.
- In 1872 the Supreme Court confirmed Presbyterian constitutional policies and ruled that in the case of property used for religious services or ecclesiastical purposes in the Presbyterian church, the trustees are under the authority of the session (which is itself under the authority of the presbytery, synod, and General Assembly). In 1874 the General Assembly charged the session with the supervision of all of the spiritual interests of the congregation and declared that any action by the trustees, unauthorized by the congregation, is illegal and void. This action was reaffirmed by the General Assembly in 1893. These rulings were necessitated because of the number of complaints lodged over the years against the unwarranted use of power by trustees in violation of the *Constitution* of the church.

As the *Book of Order* currently states this principle, the session has the authority "to delegate and to supervise the work of the board of deacons and the board of trustees and all other organizations and task forces within the congregation, providing for support, report, review, and control" (G-10.0102m).

- Trustees could be elected or appointed, depending on the polity of the church in question. In Presbyterian churches today they are normally nominated by the congregational nominating committee and elected by the congregation (G-14.0201b), usually at the annual meeting. The trustees will be elders serving on the session "unless the corporation shall determine another method" (G-7.0401), for example, electing a separate board of trustees or having the deacons serve that function.

- Prior to the inclusion of women as church members and their election as officers, only adult men could serve as trustees; in many communities they had to be citizens and registered voters. In the PC(USA) both men and women are eligible to hold all church offices (G-6.0105). As in the case of the election of deacons and elders, all nominations for office should give "fair representation to persons of all age groups and of all racial ethnic members and persons with disabilities who are members of that congregation" (G-14.0201b).

- In the former UPCNA and the PCUSA the congregation and the corporation were considered to be separate legal entities, and their meetings had to be held at separate times, even if one meeting merely followed immediately after the other. Some churches still continue this tradition, even though most states no longer require it. When civil law does require that corporate business be conducted in a separate corporate meeting of the congregation, such a meeting is called by the trustees or at their discretion, or when directed by the session or the presbytery (G-7.0403a). In such a case the trustees shall designate a presiding officer and a secretary from among members on the active roll of the church.

Indeed, the varying functions of trustees in different states were significant enough to be mentioned prominently in *A Manual for Ruling Elders and Church Sessions*, a guide in use in different editions in the PCUSA for many years prior to the reorganization of the church in 1958.

> The powers conferred upon church trustees by the laws of the different States vary from full authority to manage, down to mere title-holding. Care should be taken, therefore, to ascertain in each State the exact powers given to the trustees. In many of the States, . . . the trustees of religious societies are simply the title-holders to property, and have no independent authority and disposition. That management and disposition are vested in the congregation. The trustees, however, should be authorized to provide for the care of property and the payment of church expenses.[10]

In some states it is still the case that the only responsibility of the trustees is to hold title and manage the church's property. Their election by the congregation may require confirmation by the local Circuit Court, and churches uncertain about local laws should consult with a knowledgeable state attorney or the presbytery.

In many churches, especially in the southern states, the trustee duties, especially financial responsibilities, were given to the board of deacons. In the PCUS, for example, the deacons were specifically assigned the duties reserved for trustees elsewhere: to develop the gift of liberality; to develop, in collaboration with the session, the use of offerings; to plan effective methods for taking collections; to keep church property in proper repair; and so forth.[11] According to our current *Constitution*, deacons may continue to carry out these functions in churches that choose this organizational model (G-6.0406).[12]

Questions for Study

1. What should the proper relationship be between church law and local, state, and federal regulations? Do you think that secular laws should be able to regulate religious institutions? Or should the principle that rulings of ecclesiastical bodies cannot be subject to legal review prevail? What does the First Amendment mean to your congregation in practical terms?

2. Do you think that state and federal governments should be able to give grants to religious institutions for

charitable work or is that a violation of the separation of church and state?

3. Do you think that churches should continue to be exempt from taxes when local and state budgets are facing huge deficits?

4. How are the trustees organized in your own congregation? Which historic tradition does your organization of trustee responsibilities reflect?

Chapter 3

The Responsibilities and Powers of Trustees

The Church as a Corporation

According to the *Book of Order* every congregation, whenever permitted by civil law, shall cause a corporation to be formed and maintained (G-7.0401).[1] The directors of the corporation shall be members of a board of trustees elected by the corporation, elders serving on the session, or deacons appointed by the session (G-6.0406).

The "trustee corporation," in contrast to the "corporation sole" (where management and control is vested in one person, typically a bishop), is one in which the officers elected by the church hold property in trust for the body and exercise other powers as granted by state or ecclesiastical laws. Although the trustees make up the corporation, they can act only in accordance with the laws of the religious body of which they are a part.[2]

The Management of Property

In the Presbyterian Church (U.S.A.) the trustees, as officers of the corporation, have the following powers (G-7.0402):

- to receive, hold, encumber, manage and transfer property, real or personal, for the church
- to accept and execute deeds of title to such property
- to hold and defend title to such property
- to manage any permanent special funds for the furtherance of the purposes of the church, all subject to the provisions of the *Constitution of the PC(USA)*, provided further that in buying, selling, and mortgaging real property, the trustees shall act only after approval is granted in a duly constituted congregational meeting (G-7.0402; 8.0500).

As trustees assume their powers to administer the property of the church, they must always remember that theirs is primarily a legal and advisory responsibility. In the PC(USA) the session always has the final authority to supervise the work of the trustees (G-10.0102m; 7.0401). Any recommendations that are made in regard to changes in the rental, leasing, or ownership of property must be approved, furthermore, by the congregation at a called meeting (G-7.0304a[4]) and by the written permission of the presbytery transmitted through the session (G-8.0501). Although the trustees often recommend and carry out policies for the use of the church plant, only the session has the power "to provide for the management of the property of the church, including determination of the appropriate use of church buildings and facilities" (G-10.0102o).

In regard to the rental or conveyance of property, it is recommended that the trustees be in conversation with the appropriate committee of the presbytery in the early stages of negotiation, in order to benefit from the experience and wisdom of the members of the presbytery and ensure that the proper steps are taken to gain the approval of that governing body later. The General Assembly Council Office of Legal/Risk Management Services provides an excellent outline of suggested steps in the *Legal Resource Manual for Presbyterian Church (U.S.A.) Middle Governing Bodies and Churches*. Included are guidelines for the preparation of the contract of conveyance, the delivery of the conveyancing instrument (usually a deed), and the responsibility of the presbytery to make sure that the property is free of any encumbrances.[3] Regarding the purchase of buildings, the manual provides recommendations about the obtaining of warranties in purchase contracts in reference to the soundness of the structure, compliance with local building codes, pest and termite infestations, and so forth.

The corporation of the particular church will adopt resolutions that direct and authorize the corporation's board of directors [the trustees] to execute the necessary papers, i.e., contracts of sale, deeds, leases, bills of sale, mortgages, etc. The corporation's board of directors must also adopt any resolutions as necessary or required by local law and the corporation's bylaws. Any written instruments, i.e., contracts, deeds, bills of sale, mortgages etc., necessary to carry out the action as authorized are to be executed in the name of the corporation by its authorized officers. Upon execution, these instruments are binding and effective as the action of the corporation.[4]

The General Assembly of the PC(USA) provides two loan programs to help churches meet the needs for capital funds, the Church Loan Program, and the Investment and Loan Program. The first is funded by endowments and by accumulated designated mission funds given for this purpose. The source of the second is investments made by individuals, congregations, governing bodies, and other related groups in the PC(USA). All loans are made at affordable rates.[5]

When major capital repairs or building projects are being anticipated, the trustees, with session approval, may also explore the excellent services offered by the CFCS (Church Financial Campaign Service of the Presbyterian Church (U.S.A.)). Their expert campaign directors have experience in working with all sizes of congregations and churches in many different locales and areas of the country and will help develop a fund-raising plan at a modest cost that is just right for any particular church.[6]

The Trustee as an Officer of the Whole Church

Some Presbyterians may wonder why trustees must gain approval of the presbytery prior to loans, rentals, and sales of church property if they are the officers of the corporation. The *Constitution* makes it clear that a trustee does more than serve one congregation: he or she is responsible to the whole church in the name of Jesus Christ. As Presbyterians we do not exist as a solitary congregation in a local community but as a part of a nationwide church that is united under one *Constitution* containing the *Book of Order* and the *Book of Confessions*. As the *Form of Government* states it,

> All property held by or for a particular church, a presbytery, a synod, the General Assembly, or the Presbyterian Church (U.S.A.), whether legal title is lodged in a corporation, a trustee or trustees, or an unincorporated association, and whether the property is used in programs of a particular church or of a more inclusive governing body or retained for the production of income, is held in trust nevertheless for the use and benefit of the Presbyterian Church (U.S.A.) (G-8.0201).

The words "held in trust" are critical. They indicate that legally the church buildings, property, cash, and investments do not belong finally to the church members or the corporation in a particular city, town, or village, but to all Presbyterians across the nation, that is, to the whole denomination. Since Presbyterians have accepted principles of

Reformed theology, mission, and polity since the sixteenth century, the trustees or session of a congregation do not have the legal or spiritual authority to change the practices of a church so that the church is no longer recognizable as Presbyterian and Reformed.

The property of a congregation can be used only in ways that are consistent with the mission and practices described in the *Constitution* of the PC(USA). The session and board of trustees must always be careful not only that members are engaging in activities that are compatible with our mission and polity but that outside groups that use the buildings and grounds of the church are also engaging in practices that are congruous with the faith and mission of the PC(USA) and principles of the Reformed tradition. Thus, to use extreme examples, a church that shows pornographic movies, violates the rights of children and youth, or discriminates against members of the community for reasons of sex, ethnic background, age, or disability could be found in violation of the church's *Constitution*. If it is determined that church buildings are used in inappropriate ways, "such property shall be held, used, applied, transferred, or sold as provided by the presbytery" (G-8.0301).

This central principle is well stated in a *Manual for Ruling Elders and Other Church Officers,* first published in 1897:

In connection with the whole subject of the uses of church property, it is important to bear in mind that every religious society or church is, in the eye of the civil law, a voluntary association, and that such associations have the right to determine their own rules and usages. This right has been repeatedly recognized by the civil courts, and especially in the case of religious societies. Further, where a congregation is affiliated with a denomination, the laws and usages of the denomination are in force in the congregation, and cannot be set to one side. For this reason the deliverances of the General Assembly have an important bearing on the powers of the trustees. Where the civil law is silent, the ecclesiastical law is operative.[7]

Although individual churches have the right and responsibility to use imagination and creativity in their worship, programs, and mission activities, the tradition of our faith and practice is important too. "The Presbyterian system of government calls for continuity with and faithfulness to the heritage which lies behind the contemporary church" (G-4.0303).

Normally this provision of the *Constitution* is rarely noticed or invoked. Most of the time congregations function peacefully as part of the whole body. The pastors and the elders elected by the session attend presbytery meetings, and there is no need to consider who has final authority over property and programs. In the rare cases, however, when a church espouses beliefs or pursues policies that are antithetical to the Reformed tradition and the *Constitution*, the presbytery does have the right, after the application of procedures outlined in the *Form of Government* and *Rules of Discipline*, to seize property and assets. Two passages in the *Form of Government* outline this authority clearly:

> A higher governing body shall have the right of review and control over a lower one and shall have power to determine matters of controversy upon reference, complaint, or appeal. (G-4.0301f)

> Governing bodies possess whatever administrative authority is necessary to give effect to duties and powers assigned by the Constitution of the church. (G-4.0301i)

The absence of a trust clause in a conveyance instrument (a statement prohibiting a church from taking the property with them if they leave the denomination) does not alter the responsibility of a congregation, session, church agency, or corporate board to a presbytery, synod, or the denomination (G-8.0000). When evidence exists that a particular church has been a member church of the denomination,

> secular courts have upheld the right of denominational units to succeed to the title on the implied trust theory. It is extremely important to understand that, although title to the property may be held by a particular church subject to the provisions of the Constitution, the title is merely held in trust for the denomination by that entity. The title may be taken in the name of the corporation of certain trustees but the Constitution clearly states that *all*

such properties are held in trust for the denomination, whether or not a trust clause is included in the instrument of conveyance.[8]

Rental or Leasing of Church Property

Although the local church has the authority to lease or rent its property, restrictions that apply demonstrate how the principle "held in trust" works out practically. According to the *Book of Order* (G-8.0502), "A particular church shall not lease its real property used for purposes of worship, or lease for more than five years any of its other real property, without the written permission of the presbytery transmitted through the session of the particular church." "Used for worship" refers to the sanctuary, a chapel, or any other rooms used by the congregation in its regular services. Thus if the session and/or trustees desire to rent the sanctuary to another denominational group or Presbyterian congregation on Sunday afternoon or some evening during the week, prior presbytery approval must be received before a lease is signed. The trustees may recommend the use of other parts of the church plant for office space (for a presbytery or charitable organization, for example), or for educational use (a day care center, a Christian school, fitness center, etc.), or for meeting or worship purposes. All such leases must be approved by the session. The approval of presbytery is required when the time limit stated above is exceeded. Nevertheless it is wise to consult with the appropriate presbytery committees in all cases to make sure that requirements for property tax exemption and property and liability insurance are being met, and that all zoning ordinances and fire codes are being observed.

Property of a Dissolved or Extinct Church

The *Book of Order* makes provision for the sale of church property whenever a congregation is formally dissolved by the presbytery (G-8.0400). A church may close because of the absence of a working membership or the abandonment of the work of the congregation. In all cases the church must work directly with the presbytery: "such property as it may have shall be held, used, and applied for such uses, purposes, and trusts as presbytery may direct, limit, and appoint, or such property may be sold or disposed of as the presbytery may direct, . . . in conformity with the *Constitution of the Presbyterian Church (U.S.A.)*" (G-8.0401).

Generally the church will be working with the presbytery's committee on ministry, and/or the committee of strategic planning, or the presbytery trustees and attorney to make decisions about the proper sale or disposal, not only of buildings, but of contents, equipment, church heirlooms, financial assets, and so on.[9] Normally all financial funds, endowments, and gifts will be retained by the presbytery. If possible, it is advisable to postpone the dissolution of the congregation and maintain the existence of the corporation and the board of trustees until all legal issues have been resolved. This allows the trustees to continue to function as officers of the corporation. If this is not possible, the presbytery fulfills these functions.

"When property is of minimum value and/or a buyer is difficult to find, it may be better to transfer the property for nominal consideration rather than having the responsibility to maintain and insure the property. One solution for a cemetery is to transfer the property to a local cemetery association composed of individuals with family buried there."[10] In all cases, an attorney should be consulted.

A Church in Schism

When there is a sharp disagreement or a schism within a particular congregation, its relationship to the PC(USA) can be severed only by action of the presbytery. If it is impossible to effect a reconciliation, the presbytery has the authority to decide if one of the factions is entitled to the property because it is determined that it is the true church within the denomination. Such a determination is not based on which faction within the church received the majority vote at the time of the division (G-8.0601) but on the presbytery's judgment concerning issues involving conformity to the *Book of Order*, theological affirmation of the *Book of*

Confessions, and the proper use of liturgical practices according to the *Directory for Worship*.

Historic Landmark Designations

Churches that are currently on the National Register of Historic Sites should consult local regulations before changes are made to the exterior of their buildings. Often, structures that are of important historic or cultural significance are not allowed to be altered without approval from the appropriate municipal boards or committees.[11]

The board of trustees or session needs to examine the pros and cons of the historic landmarking of churches if the church has not already entered into such an agreement. Since the provisions of such laws are usually determined by local governments, even though it is possible to secure good advice about historic preservation from landmark societies, and even though financial assistance in the form of grants is occasionally available, such a designation also has disadvantages. A landmark society or historic preservation committee may block projected repairs to the facade of buildings or to signage. Fines may be imposed on the owners of buildings that are in disrepair.[12] In addition, many communities will not permit external changes, the erection of signs, or new lighting, and so on, without the approval of zoning boards and/or historic preservation committees, whether the buildings are registered or not. Before any proposed changes approach the final planning stages, make a careful study of local building and fire code ordinances.

Other Duties

In addition to these primary responsibilities regarding the administration of property, trustees in many churches, especially where there are bicameral boards, are also authorized by the session to take on other important tasks:

- serving as the maintenance committee of the church
- monitoring the church budget
- assisting in the formulation of long-range capital goals
- serving on or administering investment and endowment committees
- selecting and reviewing insurance policies
- supervising custodial and/or office personnel
- selecting and maintaining computer, audiovisual, photographic, and telephone equipment
- monitoring building security
- maintaining inventories
- helping to secure legal representation for congregation and staff

BUILDINGS AND GROUNDS

In congregations that have bicameral boards the trustees usually have a buildings and grounds committee. The responsibilities of such a group may involve the following:

1. the maintenance of all church buildings
2. the repair or replacement of equipment
3. planning for long-term maintenance projects
4. the organization of work groups that meet to do periodic cleaning, painting, and installation of new equipment such as lights, telephones, computers, smoke and heat alarms, thermostats, and so forth
5. supervision of custodial staff and establishment of regular cleaning schedules
6. inspections of buildings and equipment
7. maintenance and development of lawns, flower beds, sidewalks, driveways, parking lots, cemeteries, and memorial gardens
8. supervision of snow-plowing, lawn-mowing, or other contracts

CHURCH BUDGET

Although the session is responsible for the establishment of the congregational budget and the distribution of all mission funds (G-10.0102i), in many churches the elders and trustees work together closely in the planning of the annual challenge budget (a preliminary report that reflects the anticipated needs of the church before pledges are received) and the monitoring of the final budget with monthly financial reports.

One possible approach to the challenge is to ask all committees and boards to prepare financial plans for the next year in May or June. These figures are then examined by a representative budget committee composed of session members, trustees, deacons, members of the various church committees, and members at large. A prospective (challenge) budget is presented to the session in June or September and, after session approval, is available for interpretation by the stewardship committee for the annual pledge drive in early fall. The session approves the final budget for the next year after the pledges are received.

Trustees are an important part of this process, since the maintenance and repair of church property usually comprises a high percentage of the annual budget. Trustees, moreover, may have extensive experience in financial planning. Frequently the church treasurer attends meetings of the board of trustees and may be a member of that board (G-10.0401). The session may give the board of trustees the responsibility to supervise his or her work.

LONG-RANGE CAPITAL GOALS

Trustees may work closely with the session on the development of long-range capital goals as the church plans ahead to renovate a sanctuary, repair or replace an organ, refurbish kitchen and dining areas, remodel educational rooms, or build additions. When expensive projects or widespread rearrangement of rooms in the church is considered, it is often wise to have joint meetings between the session and the board of trustees where brainstorming about construction possibilities and fund-raising plans can take place.

It is also wise to consider the establishment of separate escrow accounts to finance the maintenance of new equipment such as elevators, heating and air conditioning systems, voice mail centers, computers, and copiers, or to provide for custodial service, utility costs, and insurance for new buildings. Some institutions make sure that the cost of future upkeep is included in the original budgetary or capital improvement fund-raising proposals. If an elevator is projected to cost $100,000 to purchase and install, for example, the session and trustees may budget $115,000 so that the extra $15,000 earns interest each year to cover the expense of mandated annual inspections and routine maintenance contracts. Without financial planning of this nature, each new purchase adds unforeseen expense to the church's annual budget and can eventually lead to runaway costs no longer covered by pledges or endowment income.

INVESTMENT AND ENDOWMENT COMMITTEES

Trustees are often given the responsibility to develop and maintain the investments and endowments owned by the congregation. It is important to create an investment strategy (with the approval of the session) that reflects the congregation's financial needs and investment goals. Pertinent questions might include the following:

- How does the congregation expect to use investments and endowments?

- Do the session and congregation understand the legal restrictions imposed by the donor of an endowment, gift, or bequest, if there are any? If the donor specifies how the gift is to be used, whether or not the principal may be invaded, how the interest is to be used, to whom it must be given, and so on, these guidelines obligate the congregation legally, and there can be costly consequences if they are ignored.
- Who will make the decision about how, where, and when investments will be made? Will the session have a special committee to make these recommendations? Will there be a broadly representative endowment committee? Will the trustees take on this task with session approval? What will be the principles of investment be? How are potential conflicts of interest between various boards going to be avoided?
- Is the principal going to be drawn down to maintain the annual budget in future years? What percentage of the principal is to be used in such a way? What formula will be used to determine what this percentage should be?
- What will happen to church financial prospects if all investments are depleted and the portfolio is entirely emptied?
- Is the principal to remain invested in perpetuity with only interest available for expenditures?
- Should a portion of the interest income be reinvested to keep pace with inflationary costs or downturns in

the economy? What formula will be used to determine what that portion will be?

- What kind of investments is the church willing to make? What kind should it make? What kinds of endowments is it willing to accept as gifts?
- Do church officers want to consider the purchase of stock in any corporations that will provide a profit, or do they want to restrict investments to corporations that are socially responsible? Would the church invest in companies that make weapons and munitions or would that be considered unethical? Would the church continue to hold stock in a company that sells unhealthy products, exploits foreign and domestic workers, or is involved in fraudulent behavior? How should a congregation use its voting power as a stockholder to influence corporate policies? Guidance about these important questions can be secured from MRTI (Mission Responsibility Through Investment) in Louisville. Both the UPCUSA (1971) and the PCUS (1976) recognized the need to recognize investment as an instrument of mission that includes theological, social, and economic considerations, and their different emphases were combined in the Structural Design for Mission approved by the General Assembly in 1986. For information, visit the MRTI website: www.pcusa.org/mrti.
- How will monetary gifts and endowments be used? Many churches design a policy statement to be distributed to potential donors that illustrates how gifts

will be utilized. For example, it might be decided that gifts or endowment interest will be used only according to the following guidelines:

25% for the church's annual budget
25% for new mission projects
10% for reinvestment
15% for new capital improvement projects
25% for new programs in the local congregation

Such a statement of purpose informs donors that a plan is in place, makes it clear who has the responsibility to spend funds, and reassures them that their gifts will be used carefully and wisely.

The questions about endowment and investment policy are complex and can be answered only after careful prayer, discussion, and research. As these and other policies are determined, they can be summarized in a comprehensive church investment and endowment policy statement that can be used to interpret the plans and purposes of the church. It is wise to consult with a financial counselor, a brokerage firm, and presbytery trustees to consider all the options.

Many churches and presbyteries utilize the excellent services of the Presbyterian Church (U.S.A.) Foundation for advice about investment and promotional plans. The Foundation also provides investment opportunities for money raised through gifts, bequests, sale of stocks and bonds, and deferred giving.[13] Established more than two hundred years ago, the Foundation assists individuals with decisions about gift annuities, pooled income funds, revocable life income funds, annuity trusts, and wills and bequests. It also assists churches by providing planned giving consultations, training and education programs, seminars and workshops, and so forth.

SELECTING AND REVIEWING INSURANCE POLICIES

The board of trustees and/or session is responsible for the selection of all the congregation's insurance policies and periodic review of property insurance, general liability, professional and sexual liability insurance for pastors and other staff, worker's compensation, coverage for church groups traveling on trips approved by session, bonding policies for financial staff and officers, and so on (G-10.0102o). Churches may contract with local insurance companies or may discover that substantial savings may be realized by using one of the three insurance companies profiled by the General Assembly–level offices of the PCUSA: Church Mutual Insurance, Covenant Presbyterian Insurance, and Guideline Insurance.[14] It is often possible to benefit from master policies created by a presbytery or synod in which cost benefits and coverages are provided that are unavailable to individual congregations.

SUPERVISING CUSTODIAL AND/OR OFFICE PERSONNEL

In many churches the supervision of custodial and office personnel is one of the responsibilities of the board of trustees. In a large congregation the session's personnel committee may need to focus attention on pastoral, educational, and music staff while the trustees work with employees dealing more directly with their range of duties. In smaller congregations the trustees may oversee the custodian, secretary, and financial secretary in order to free the pastors from day-to-day oversight. The trustees or members of the buildings and grounds committee are often best suited to design a weekly cleaning schedule for the custodian and to monitor the work being done, since they are the officers most familiar with the church's schedules, the layout of church buildings, and routine maintenance.

SELECTING AND MAINTAINING EQUIPMENT

In the course of a congregation's life many decisions have to be made concerning the purchase of necessary equipment such as lawn mowers, snow blowers, furnaces, air conditioners, vacuum cleaners, floor polishers, telephone systems, computers, copy machines, fire extinguishers, projectors, smoke and fire detectors, audiovisual equipment, cleaning supplies, refrigerators, industrial-size stoves, paint products, thermostats, and so forth. These purchases can be expedited if the trustees establish a procedure of needs assessment, bidding processes, and a means to determine whether payments should be made by cash or by an installment plan. Trustees can also assume the responsibilities of comparing prices, researching the quality of different products, determining the proper warranties to be selected, and purchasing necessary long-term maintenance contracts.

The trustees can take on the duty of establishing an inventory list of equipment, furniture, and supplies in every church room (with photographs or videos if possible), developing a maintenance schedule for equipment owned, and designing a long-range plan for the replacement of high-ticket items such as boilers, roofs, copiers, parking lots, and sidewalks.[15]

BUILDING SECURITY

In recent years it has become painfully clear that all churches must be aware of the critical need for careful building security. Some members and pastors may remember times when this was not the case. In my first church, members were upset when the sanctuary could no longer be left open twenty-four hours a day for prayer and meditation. Frequent robberies and vandalism forced them to change their perspective. Other members were insulted when I insisted on locking the doors of my house because they took an Old West pride in the fact that all of their neighbors were honest and trustworthy. "We never had a robbery on our road for fifty years," they boasted. Apparently it had not occurred to them that even if all their neighbors were upstanding (I had my doubts about a few of them), it was still possible for thieves from other towns to drive over (or ride a horse) and burgle their wide-open homes.

Today no one doubts the necessity for careful security systems, and trustees and elders must work closely with security experts to protect buildings and property. One of the biggest problems churches face is the widespread proliferation of church keys among church members and other people in the community who have used the facility in the past. Congregants often joke that half the city has a key to the side door already, so why bother to lock it? In order to protect personnel who have to work in our offices, and to secure valuable computer equipment, communion ware, offering plates, candlesticks, organs, and other musical instruments, today's trustees must consider at least one or all of three possibilities:

- the changing of church locks and the issuance of keys only to current staff and selected officers
- the installation of a computerized security system that can be opened only with proper identification cards or by punching a security code into an external panel
- the installation of an electronic alarm system that is connected to a police station or a professional security company

Churches also frequently face the danger of theft, malicious destruction, and arson because members and outside groups using the church facilities forget to secure buildings after meetings. In order to protect occupants and maintain insurance requirements, trustees may need to take steps that increase the budget modestly now but save overwhelming expenses in the future. Options include the paying of a custodian to check the buildings at regular daily intervals to make sure that all windows and doors are locked, the hiring of a local security firm to inspect the premises, and the installation of electronic locks that automatically lock at preset times.

SECURING LEGAL REPRESENTATION

In the litigious society in which we live it is often necessary to engage the services of an attorney who is familiar with the legal needs of the local church, the *Book of Order*, and local and state laws. Many situations can arise in which legal advice may be needed: the purchase or selling of property; liability claims filed by people using church buildings; the examination and maintenance of contracts with architects, contractors, and service providers; advising members about wills and bequests; the development of building usage policies for outside groups; claims against the congregation by disgruntled employees. Some churches are fortunate to have legal services offered pro bono by members who are attorneys. Advice may also be obtained from counselors who serve the presbytery. In extreme cases it may be necessary to keep an attorney on retainer to protect the interests of the congregation, staff, and officers of the corporation. When the church or its officers are sued, the insurance company should be notified promptly. Often, the insurance policy provides for payment of attorneys' fees in the defense of claims. Sometimes the insurance company will work with the church in selection of the attorney.

CHAIRPERSON OF THE BOARD OF TRUSTEES

According to the *Book of Order* (G-7.0403) the trustees shall elect a minimum of two officers, a presiding officer (often given the title of chairperson or president) and a secretary. The chairperson's duties differ in various congregations, but generally he or she presides at the meetings of the board, works with the pastor(s) to set the agenda, makes appointments on the board's behalf, and may have the responsibility of signing legal documents and contracts as the president of the corporation. Generally the chairperson is elected annually.

It is in the church's best interests for the chairperson to be kept informed as much as possible about the decisions of the session (he or she may be invited regularly to stated meetings) and to be included on central committees that develop recommendations about finances, investments, capital improvements, and long-range planning. If the chairperson is "in the loop," it is easier to maintain healthy and positive communication among the trustees, staff members, and other officers. In most congregations the chairperson meets regularly with the pastor, the financial secretary, and the church treasurer to share information and facilitate planning.

CHURCH TREASURER

The church treasurer is elected annually by the session (G-10.0401) and may be supervised by that board or by the trustees or deacons, as the session decides. Generally the treasurer is responsible for the supervision of financial staff members, arranging the mandated annual financial review (G-10.0401d), monitoring the regular payment of bills, overseeing the fulfillment of contracts, providing for the counting of all offerings by at least two duly appointed persons or a fidelity bonded individual (G-10.0401a), preparing monthly budget reports, and maintaining checking and saving accounts. He or she needs to work regularly with the pastor in order to keep abreast of opportunities and problems in the church and current session policies.[16]

Questions for Study

1. How do you assign the tasks of the trustees in your congregation? If you have a bicameral system, how do you maintain communication between the session and the board of trustees? How do you resolve possible differences of opinion or conflicts of interest? If you have a unicameral board, how are the responsibilities of the trustees assigned to session committees? Could your organizational system be improved?

2. When your church is considering major budget changes or capital improvements, do you consult with the

members of the church through congregational meetings, or does the session make the decisions? What are the advantages and disadvantages of including the congregation in such discussions? When the congregation is required to vote on the sale of property, the mortgaging, encumbering, or leasing of property, how do you go about informing the members of the church beforehand?

3. Do you know what the endowment policies of your church are? How much are your endowment and/or savings accounts worth? Are there any restrictions about how these monies may be spent?

4. Do you have any long-term plans for financing the repair and replacement of roofs, boilers, computers, copiers, or other major structures or pieces of equipment? If not, how do you plan to pay for such expenses when they inevitably occur?

Chapter 4

Professional Ethics and Standards of Conduct

A question that all trustees will need to ask themselves in the twenty-first century is foundational. It springs from the basic definition of their office. "Are we trustworthy?" If trustees truly are spiritual officers of the church, and their calling is derived from the gifts of the Holy Spirit that are enumerated by Paul in 1 Corinthians 12 (see chapter 1),[1] then the admonition given to deacons, elders, and pastors in the *Book of Order* applies to them as well (G-6.0106a).

> In addition to possessing the necessary gifts and abilities, natural and acquired, those who undertake particular ministries should be persons of strong faith, dedicated discipleship, and love of Jesus Christ as Savior and Lord. Their manner of life should be a demonstration of the Christian gospel in the church and the world.

In his book on the ethical integrity required of church officers Paul Chaffee focuses on accountability:

> Accountability is the obligation one assumes in accepting the prerogative to lead the community in one way or the other, make decisions, and act in its behalf. . . . Basic standards of accountability spring to mind when we consider what is expected of a good leader. The confidence that congregations rest in leaders assume that they will be faithful, informed, honest, fair, and responsible.[2]

In its most fundamental sense, being accountable means being professional, aboveboard, legal, doing the right thing all the time. As the old adage puts it, although there are hundreds of ways to mislead, cheat, steal, and defraud, there is only one way to be honest.

What is demanded of the Presbyterian trustee goes even beyond the highest levels of ethical conduct required of business executives, important as they are. A church officer is committed to Jesus Christ and takes Paul's charge in Colossians 3:17, often used in installation services, with absolute seriousness: "And whatever you do, in word or deed, do everything in the name of the Lord Jesus, giving thanks to God the Father through him."[3]

Chaffee points to a number of key ethical characteristics that an accountable officer must have:

- always works for the best interests of the community
- is aware of the power of his or her role and lives

consistently within the ethical boundaries that make up church authority
- is aware of the rules of the community and state and federal laws and obeys them
- tells the truth
- abstains from taking personal gain when dealing with the financial matters of the church[4]

A few examples will make the point clear. In regard to the purchasing of products for use in the church, the board of trustees and the session must be adamant in the resolve to seek multiple bids and assure that the church obtains the fairest bid possible. Although it is tempting to buy from a church member or an acquaintance because he/she has offered a price break in the past, and because officers usually want to support local businesses, the use of a typical three-bid requirement removes all suggestions of favoritism or insider deals. Of course, the lowest price is not necessarily the best choice, especially if an inferior product is offered, or the company involved is suspected of illegal actions or unjust labor practices. Church officers must consider many factors before a bid is finally accepted.

The same is true of the letting of contracts in the church for repairs, construction, snow removal, lawn maintenance, the paving of parking lots, and so on. An open bidding process informs members of the church and the community that all business is conducted in a professional and fair manner.

The *Book of Order* provides another example when it requires the proper accounting of all cash contributions and pledge payments. The minimum standards include the following (G-10.0400):

- the counting and recording of all offerings by at least two duly appointed persons or a fidelity bonded individual
- the keeping of adequate books and records to reflect all financial transactions, open to inspection by all authorized church officers at reasonable times
- periodic reporting of the financial activities to the board or boards vested with financial authority, at least annually, preferably more often

In addition to these requirements it is prudent to have the pastor(s) and all church officers scrupulously avoid the handling of any cash given to the church. Even money donated at a church supper or given to pay for a book ordered for an adult class should be counted by two people, properly recorded, and handed to the financial secretary or church treasurer in a sealed envelope to avoid any hint of fiscal impropriety.

As a nonprofit corporation the church must also take care to exercise the privilege of its tax-exempt status with complete integrity. Only products and services used for legitimate church business should be purchased under the tax-exempt number. This advantage should not be extended under any circumstances to staff members or officers in order to save them money for private purchases. Such a practice, regardless of the rationalizations given, is illegal.[5] Thus the pastor cannot use the tax-exempt number to buy a new suit, purchase airline tickets for vacation, or acquire electronic equipment for the manse with the vague excuse that these items might somehow be used in his or her work. The church must also keep records of all profits made from activities that are not strictly related to the congregation's mission. In some cases, taxes must be paid on income not related to the nonprofit purposes of the church.

Somewhat similarly, a strict accounting must also be kept of all pastoral expenses that can be claimed as deductible and nontaxable under state and federal laws. In all cases, they must be vouchered and accompanied by a receipt from the appropriate vendor. Accounts for the nontaxable portions of a pastor's salary (car allowance, housing allowance, professional expenses, study leave, etc.) must be established at the beginning of each calendar year and approved by the session and the congregation (G-7.0302a; 14.0506b). They cannot be endorsed as an afterthought by the session or board of trustees in July or October.

The ethical behavior of church officers should always be expected to be of the very highest caliber and conform to the requirements of local, state, and federal laws. Recent revelations of sexual misconduct by clergy and church officers, both Roman Catholic and Protestant, have eroded public confidence in the integrity of all who serve the church.[6] Pastors, elders, deacons, and trustees must be aware of the fact that what they do speaks more loudly than what they preach or say. Their lives and their conduct inside and outside of the congregation reflect directly on the mission of the church of Jesus Christ. They provide examples of the Christian life to children, to other church members, and to the community (1 Thess. 1:7; 2 Thess. 3:9; Phil. 3:17). People outside the congregation reasonably expect us to obey the Ten Commandments; to be temperate, sensible, and respectable (1 Tim. 3:2); and to follow in the footsteps of our Lord Jesus Christ (1 Pet. 2:21; 1 Cor. 11:1; 1 Tim. 1:16).

The advice given to young men by the author of Titus applies especially to those who are called to witness to Christ through the way in which they administer the church. "Show yourself in all respects a model of good works, and . . . show integrity, gravity, and sound speech that cannot be censured" (Titus 2:7). A manual published many years ago by the former Presbyterian Board of Education focuses attention on the trustee's primary obligation.

[I]t is a major responsibility of the board of trustees to conduct the business of the church in such a way as to make a witness for Christian ethical standards. The church must not undercut its influence by conducting its own affairs in a way contrary to its essential message.[7]

Questions for Study

1. What do you think it means for trustees to be trustworthy today? Can you think of any ways in which you have changed your behavior or your habits since you became a church officer?

2. Have you ever seen church boards adopt unethical practices in making purchases or developing contracts? Have you ever paid suppliers or employees under the table? Do you know of church boards that have taken a stand against such practices, even if it might cost them money or prestige or make them liable to legal penalties?

3. How is money counted in your congregation? Who does it? How is it recorded? How are pledges tallied? How often are reports sent to members of the congregation? How often does the session or board of trustees report to the congregation about financial decisions that are being considered? How often should they report?

4. Who makes up the monthly financial report in your church? How is auditing done? When is the last time your books were audited by an accountant or a professional accounting firm? Have you ever tracked a few line items over a period of a few months to see if they are being calculated accurately? Who balances bank statements for the

church? How often are they done? What safeguards do you have against employee or officer embezzlement?

5. What action would your trustees take if an officer or staff member were suspected of stealing from the church?

Chapter 5

Future Prospects: Administering Christ's Church with Justice

As we strain to look ahead and ascertain what form the Presbyterian church might take later in the twenty-first century, what can trustees visualize about the responsibilities and opportunities that may present themselves to those who are called by Christ to administer the church in his name?

One obligation that will increasingly be evident in the years to come moves quickly beyond the important demand for high standards of personal conduct to the critical biblical and theological vision that believers everywhere must pursue righteousness and justice for the sake of the local congregation and the world as a whole.

The *Brief Statement of Faith* in the *Book of Confessions* calls our attention to this fundamental task (C-10.65–74):

In a broken and fearful world
the Spirit gives us courage
    to pray without ceasing,

to witness among all peoples
    to Christ as Lord and Savior,
to unmask idolatries in Church and culture,
to hear the voices of peoples long silenced,
and to work with others for justice,
    freedom, and peace.
In gratitude to God, empowered by the Spirit,
    we strive to serve Christ in our daily tasks
    and to live holy and joyful lives. . . .

The *Confession of 1967* is even more prophetic and specific (C-9.46):

Because Jesus identified himself with the needy and exploited, the cause of the world's poor is the cause of his disciples. The church cannot condone poverty, whether it is the product of unjust social structures, exploitation of the defenseless, lack of natural resources, absence of technological understanding, or rapid expansion of populations.

The confession calls all believers to use their abilities, possessions, and fruits of technology as gifts entrusted to them by God for the advancement of the common welfare.

A church that is indifferent to poverty, or evades responsibilities in economic affairs, or is open to one social class only, or expects gratitude for its beneficence makes a mockery of reconciliation and offers no acceptable worship to God.

For many years Presbyterians have proclaimed that economic justice is a central feature of our administration of the church and our use of money and financial resources. As early as 1951 the UPCNA stated its conviction that

> no plea of inflation, heavy war debt or fear for our own resources can discharge the duty we have as one of the most fortunate and wealthiest nations in the world, to help feed the millions who starve in other lands today. . . . To the shallow expression, "we never had it so good," the Christian must reply, "we never had such heavy demands upon Christian conscience."[1]

In the following General Assemblies calls were made to the church and the world to ease the debt burdens of the developing nations (PCUS, 1977); to provide all the people of the world with opportunities for meaningful work and adequate food, clothing, shelter, and health care (PCUS, 1978); to divest itself of the ownership of the stocks of corporations involved in taking profit in countries that treated its citizens in unjust and inhumane ways (PC(USA), 1984); and to renew its commitment to economic justice and sustainable development, human rights, and environmental stewardship (PC(USA), 1993). In 1996 the 208th General Assembly adopted the study "Hope for a Global Future: Toward Just and Sustainable Development," which proclaimed the need for the enhancement of the quality of life for all the people of the world.

These few examples from among many[2] are sufficient to remind us that as officers of the church of Jesus Christ we are called to make decisions not just for the benefit of our congregations or the entities within our own denomination but for the prosperity of all of God's children. As Christians who are committed to God's justice, we are called to make decisions in the administration of the church that witness to God's determination to care especially for the least of our brothers and sisters.

Trustees, therefore, will need to make decisions, not just on the basis of what costs less or preserves the assets of the church, but also with God's demands for justice in mind. Where we do banking, whether or not our buildings are heated and illuminated with technology that is environmentally friendly, how we dispose of trash, where we buy our coffee, how we treat employees, how we work to preserve green space around the church, how we interact with the communities near us to support the economic and civil rights of minorities, all of these actions will be signs, not only of our business acumen, but of our faithfulness to Jesus Christ, the seriousness with which we take our mission calling to the whole world, and our determination as faithful followers to participate in his coming kingdom—not in the distant future, but today and tomorrow.

Questions for Study

1. What do you think the most pressing problems will be for trustees in the next few years? Will they be solved with justice and fairness or merely on the basis of expediency?

2. What administrative opportunities are most likely to present themselves to the church in the next few years? Will your congregation have the right officers in place to take advantage of them?

3. How does the expression "think locally, act globally" apply to the administrative decisions your trustees have to make?

4. What is your church doing now to preserve the environment? Are your heating and air-conditioning systems efficient and ecologically sound? Do you have zoned heat in all of your buildings? What kind of lights do you have? How many kilowatts do they use each month? How could you improve your church plant to save money and help preserve God's creation at the same time?

Notes

INTRODUCTION

1. See my earlier works, *Selected to Serve: A Guide for Church Officers* (Louisville, Ky.: Geneva Press, 2000); *The Presbyterian Deacon: An Essential Guide* (Louisville, Ky.: Geneva Press, 2003); and other books and manuals listed at the back of this book in "For Further Study."

CHAPTER 1

1. Anthony C. Thiselton, *The First Epistle to the Corinthians, A Commentary on the Greek Text* (Grand Rapids and Cambridge, U.K.: William B. Eerdmans Publishing Co., 2002), 1020–21.

2. Hermann Beyer, "*kubernēsis*," *Theological Dictionary of the New Testament*, vol. 3, ed. Gerhard Kittel, trans. and ed. Geoffrey W. Bromiley (Grand Rapids: William B. Eerdmans Publishing Co., 1965), 3:1035–37.

3. Gordon D. Fee, *The First Epistle to the Corinthians*, New International Commentary on the New Testament (Grand Rapids: William B. Eerdmans Publishing Co., 1987), 622, contends that Paul's use of the word contains this primary emphasis and should be translated "acts of guidance."

4. Beyer, "*kubernēsis,*" 1036.

5. Thiselton, *The First Epistle to the Corinthians*, 1021.

6. See Joseph A. Fitzmyer, *Romans, A New Translation with Introduction and Commentary*, Anchor Bible (New York: Doubleday, 1993), 750.

7. Lesley Adkins and Roy A. Adkins, *Handbook to Life in Ancient Rome* (New York and Oxford: Oxford University Press, 1994), 42.

CHAPTER 2

1. See the excellent study by Ronald H. Stone, "The Reformed Economic Ethics of John Calvin," in *Reformed Faith and Economics* (Lanham, Md., New York, and London: University Press of America, 1989), 33–48.

2. Elsie Ann McKee, *Diakonia in the Classical Reformed Tradition and Today* (Grand Rapids: William B. Eerdmans Publishing Co., 1989), 51; see 50–58 overall.

3. Stone, "Reformed Economic Ethics," 42.

4. The situation was more complex than the brief summary that follows suggests. See the detailed analysis of Derek H. Davis, *Religion and the Continental Congress 1774–1789, Contributions to Original Intent* (Oxford: Oxford University Press, 2000), esp. 27–38. Also see Gerard V. Bradley, *Church-State Relationships in America*, Contributions in Legal Stud-

ies, No. 37 (New York, Westport, Conn., and London: Greenwood Press, 1987), and Richard B. Couser, *Ministry and the American Legal System, A Guide for Clergy, Lay Workers, and Congregations* (Minneapolis: Fortress Press, 1993), 9–58.

5. Davis, *Religion and the Continental Congress*, 33.

6. *Minutes of the Presbyterian Church in America 1706–1788*, ed. Guy S. Klett (Philadelphia: Presbyterian Historical Society, 1976), 282.

7. *A Digest, Compiled From the Records of the Presbyterian Church in the United States of America, And for the Records of the Late Synod of New York and Philadelphia* (Philadelphia: Printed for the Trustees of the Assembly by R. P. McCulloh, 1820), 103.

8. Davis, *Religion and the Continental Congress*, 25, calls the approval of this principle "a revolution of monumental proportions that eventually resulted in a clean break from the European tradition that understood a common religion to be essential to the stability of the political and social order."

9. The court cases from which these examples are taken are listed by G. M. Boush, *Rulings by the Civil Courts Governing Religious Societies, A Collection of Decisions by State and Federal Courts on the Rights, Powers and Duties of Religious Societies, Their Members and Judicatories, and Their Property Rights* (Cleveland: Central Publishing House, 1915). Also see Benjamin F. Bittinger, *Manual of Law and Usage Compiled from the Standards and the Acts and Decisions of the General Assembly of the Presbyterian Church in the United States of America*, 4th ed., revised and enlarged (Philadelphia: Presbyterian Board of Publication and Sabbath-School Work,

1908), 172–75; *Manual for Church Officers of the Government, Discipline, and Worship of the Presbyterian Church in the United States of America*, 16th ed. (Philadelphia: Published for the Office of the General Assembly by the Publication Division of the Board of Christian Education of the Presbyterian Church in the United States of America, 1950), 322–52.

10. *A Manual for Ruling Elders and Church Sessions Containing the Laws and Usages of the Presbyterian Church in the U.S.A. in Relation to Ruling Elders and Other Church Officers, Church Sessions, Churches, and Congregations* (Philadelphia: Presbyterian Board of Publication and Sabbath-School Work, 1897, 1912), 382.

11. *The Book of Church Order, The Presbyterian Church in The United States* (Richmond, Va.: The Board of Education, 1968), §§ 12–13.

12. A detailed history of the role of deacons as trustees is provided in Joan S. Gray and Joyce C. Tucker, *Presbyterian Polity for Church Officers*, 3^d ed. (Louisville, Ky.: Geneva Press, 1999), 46–53. For the discussion of the broad role of deacons today, see my book *The Presbyterian Deacon*.

CHAPTER 3

1. Virginia and West Virginia did not allow churches to form corporations. In the year 2002, in *Falwell vs. Miller*, a federal district court judge overturned Article IV, Section 12 (20) of the Constitution of Virginia, which prohibits the incorporation of churches. Presbyterian congregations in Virginia will now be able to comply with the *Book of Order* under Virginia law

for corporations. The original law had its roots in the writings of Jefferson and Madison and their firm resolve to separate church and state.

2. Couser, *Ministry and the American Legal System*, 65–66.

3. *The Legal Resource Manual for Presbyterian Church (U.S.A.) Middle Governing Bodies and Churches 2000–2003* (Louisville, Ky.: General Assembly Council Office of Legal/Risk Management Services, 2000), 7–25. It is available on the website: www.pcusa.org.

4. *Legal Resource Manual*, 10. For further discussion of real estate law and the church, zoning, building codes, and issues of eminent domain, see chapter 8, "The Church As Property Owner," in Couser, *Ministry and the American Legal System*, 115–33.

5. For information, contact the Presbyterian Church (U.S.A.) Investment and Loan Program, Inc., 100 Witherspoon Street, Louisville, Ky., 40202; 800.903.7457.

6. For information, contact the Church Financial Campaign Service, 100 Witherspoon Street, Louisville, Ky. 40202; 888.219.6513.

7. *A Manual for Ruling Elders and Church Sessions,* 386.

8. *Legal Resource Manual*, 4. Emphasis is in the original text. In *Jones v. Wolf* (443US495, 606) the United States Supreme Court (1979) held that civil courts would enforce denominational property trust clauses.

9. *Legal Resource Manual*, 16–17.

10. *Legal Resource Manual*, 16.

11. For a discussion of pertinent legal cases, see Couser, *Ministry and the American Legal System*, 123–24.

12. For further discussion, see *Legal Resource Manual*, 15.

13. Presbyterian Church (U.S.A.) Foundation, 200 E. Twelfth Street, Jeffersonville, Ind. 47130; 812.288.8841.

14. See the extensive discussion of insurance coverage considerations in *Legal Resource Manual*, 111–28. Also see the website: www.pcusa.org/risk.

15. For templates of some of these responsibilities, see "Church Contents Inventory," and "Safe Conditions and Practice Survey: A Self Inspection Guide," in *Legal Resource Manual*, 123–27. For more extensive checklists, see Otto F. Crumroy Sr., Stan Kukawka, and Frank M. Witman, *Church Administration and Financial Manual: Resources for Leading the Local Church* (Harrisburg, Pa.: Morehouse Publishing, 1998), 351–62.

16. Thomas E. McLeod provides a practical outline of the treasurer's responsibilities in *The Work of the Church Treasurer*, rev. ed. (Valley Forge, Pa.: Judson Press, 1992). His chapters include "The Budget," "Cash Receipts," "Cash Disbursements," "Accounting Rules and Procedures," "Reporting," "Computer Applications," and "Software Vendors." He also provides samples of budget worksheets, monthly report forms, vouchers, member contribution records, etc.

CHAPTER 4

1. See Charles M. Olsen, *Transforming Church Boards into Communities of Spiritual Leaders* (Washington, D.C.: Alban Institute, 1995).

2. Paul Chaffee, *Accountable Leadership, A Resource Guide for Sustaining Legal, Financial, and Ethical Integrity in*

Today's Congregations (San Francisco: Jossey-Bass Publishers, 1997), 7.

3. I have explored the biblical and confessional bases of the professional ethics required in some detail in *Selected to Serve*, 141–55.

4. Chaffee, *Accountable Leadership*, 11–12.

5. See "The Presbyterian Church (U.S.A.) Group Federal 501(c)(3) Tax Exemption," *in Legal Resource Manual*, 89–90.

6. Sexual policy guidelines, complaint processes, etc. can be obtained from presbytery or synod offices. A sample policy is provided by Crumroy, Kukawka, and Witman in *Church Administration and Finance Manual*, 220–24. Also see Chaffee, *Accountable Leadership*, 185–96.

7. In *Your Church and Your Job, Elders–Deacons– Trustees* (Philadelphia: Department of Adult Work, Presbyterian Board of Christian Education, n.d.), 47–48. Also see *Understanding My Trusteeship, For Trustees* (Philadelphia: Office of Adult Work, Presbyterian Board of Education, n.d.). (These pamphlets were probably published in 1952 and 1954 respectively, but they are printed with no specific dates listed.)

CHAPTER 5

1. In *Presbyterian Social Witness Policy Compilation* (Louisville, Ky.: Advisory Committee on Social Witness Policy of the General Assembly Council, Presbyterian Church (U.S.A.), 2000), 270. References to additional General Assembly declarations are found on 271–94.

2. I have discussed many of the Presbyterian social witness statements and actions in my recent book, *Witness without*

Parallel, Eight Biblical Texts That Make Us Presbyterian (Louisville, Ky.: Geneva Press, 2003). Also see *Selected Theological Statements of the Presbyterian Church (U.S.A.) General Assemblies (1956–1998)* (Louisville, Ky.: Office of Theology and Worship, Congregational Ministries Division, Presbyterian Church (U.S.A.), 1998). Also see some of the recent issues of *Church and Society* and the articles by various authors, "Global Ethics, On the Threshold of a New Millennium," September/October 1998; "Visions for a New Century, Women and Economic Justice," January/February 2001; "The Presbyterian Church as Investor, 30 Years of Socially Responsible Investment," September/October 2002 (essays on the history of Mission Responsibility Through Investment, MRTI). For more on MRTI, see p. 44 above.

Liturgy for the Installation and Recognition of Trustees

SCRIPTURE READINGS

   Psalm 89:1–4, 13–18
   Psalm 127:1–2
   1 Corinthians 12:27–31
   Colossians 3:17

   Leader: Hands get things done.
   People: They fix the broken.
   Leader: They create the new.
   People: They comfort the brokenhearted.
   Many make work light where there are few.

   Leader: Hands hold crying children,
             dig deeply in pockets
             for those in need.
   People: They heal the sick,

mend sharp tears
in daily clothes we wear.

Leader: Hands fix and hold together
People: A world gone wrong.
Leader: They come in different forms and sizes.
People: Some are soft and supple,
applying gentle applications
of Christ's compassion.
Leader: Others, rough and calloused
by wood and nails,
do all the rugged work
God's maintenance entails.
People: They are Christ's saws and hammers,
working from God's blueprints,
building up and tearing down,
in precisely measured service.

Leader: O God, bless the trustees gathered before you
here today.
People: Bless their hands, whatever shape they take.
Leader: May their strong hands
be swift to administer the money of the people,
People: Spend and invest it wisely and honestly.

Leader: May our trustees maintain, protect, and preserve
this church's property,

People: **Being wise stewards,**
        who count the cost.

Leader: May they see our buildings
        as holy places

People: **Where the hungry are fed,**
        the thirsty given a cup,
        the wounded healed,

Leader: And the tasks of your kingdom

People: **Planned and accomplished.**

Leader: Let our trustees know,

People: **As men and women called by you,**

Leader: That unless the Lord builds the house

People: **Those who work so hard**
        labor in vain.

Leader: Let us all remember

People: **That our vocation is**
        to construct your house

Leader: And lead your people
        in Christ's mission

   All: **And that without him**
        we can do nothing.

Trustees: Even though we work with things,
          pilot the ship,
          put in the coordinates,

and set sail for horizons of the future,
we ask God to strengthen our knowledge
that Jesus Christ is our captain,
that the ship is his,
that he plots the course
and gives us orders in his service,
that he is the Head of the Body,
God's living presence in the world.

People: O God, guide them in their administrative service in Christ's name.

Trustees: O God, help us remember that we are spiritual leaders,
that we are called to serve the mission of the church,
and that all our skills and talents
come from the gifts your Spirit gives us.
May we serve you with our hands,
our skills in building and tearing down,
planning, organizing, directing, and computing,
collecting, budgeting, recording, and investing,
observing, listening, and praying.
In all things may we
always be
those who work and pray
only
to build your house.

Leader: O God, bless all our actions,
whatever form they take.
Caress us with your mercy,
move us with your strong hands.
Your arm is mighty,
strong is your hand,
held high is your right hand.

**People: You lead us by the hand,
as a parent directs the children
on the safe and prosperous way.**

Trustees: O God, righteousness and justice are foundations
of your life among us.
You strengthen us.
Steadfast love and faithfulness go before you
so that ours may be enduring witness.

**All: And now, O Lord,
we ask you to guide us
so that whatever we do,
in word or deed,
we will do everything
in the name of the Lord Jesus,
giving thanks to God through him. Amen.**

Glossary

Accommodationist. Describing a view of the United States Constitution that contends that state and local laws can regulate religions as long as they do not discriminate against particular religious groups.

Book of Confessions. The first part of the *Constitution* of the PC(USA), containing eleven Reformed confessions and creeds.

Book of Order. The second part of the *Constitution* of the PC(USA) containing the *Form of Government*, the *Directory of Worship*, and *Rules of Discipline*.

Corporation sole. A corporation whose management and control is vested in one person or group.

Disestablishment. The constitutional principal in which states support the right of religious groups to be free from governmental interference.

Establishment. The constitutional principle which grants governments certain powers over religious groups. Usually it implies financial support through tax revenues.

Forms of assistance. NRSV translation of one of Paul's terms for a gift of the Spirit in administration (1 Cor. 12:28).

Forms of Leadership. NRSV translation of one of Paul's terms for a gift of the Spirit in administration (1 Cor. 12:28).

PCUS. Presbyterian Church in the United States

PCUSA. Presbyterian Church in the United States of America (joined with the UPCNA in 1958 to form the UPCUSA)

PC(USA). Presbyterian Church (U.S.A.)

Separationist. Describing an interpretation of the United States Constitution that favors a strict separation of church and state.

Treasurer. Elected annually by the session, the officer who usually monitors the counting and recording of all offerings, the keeping of books and records, the provision of periodic budget reports, and the organization of a full annual financial review by a public accountant, public accounting firm, or a committee of members (G-10.0401).

Trustee Corporation. A corporation whose management or control is vested in a board of trustees or board of directors.

UPCNA. United Presbyterian Church in North America (joined with the PCUSA in 1958 to form the UPCUSA)

UPCUSA. United Presbyterian Church in the United States of America

For Further Study

Basic Resources

Agar, Frederick A. *Church Officers, A Study in Efficiency.* New York: Fleming H. Revell Co., 1918.

Asquith, Glenn H. *Church Officers at Work.* Philadelphia: Judson Press, 1951.

Bittinger, Benjamin F. *Manual of Law and Usage. Compiled From the Standards and the Acts and Decisions of the General Assembly of the Presbyterian Church in the United States of America.* 4th ed. Philadelphia: Presbyterian Board of Publication and Sabbath-School Work, 1908.

The Book of Church Order of the Presbyterian Church in the United States. Rev. ed. Richmond, Va.: Board of Christian Education, 1964.

Chaffee, Paul. *Accountable Leadership, A Resource Guide for Sustaining Legal, Financial, and Ethical Integrity in*

Today's Congregations. San Francisco: Jossey-Bass Publishers, 1997.

Consider Your Ministry: A Manual for New Officers of a United Presbyterian Church, Elders, Deacons, Trustees. Philadelphia: United Presbyterian Church, 1968.

Crumroy, Otto F. Sr., Stan Kukawka, and Frank M. Witman. *Church Administration and Financial Manual, Resources for Leading the Local Church.* Harrisburg, Pa.: Morehouse Publishing, 1998.

Gray, Joan S., and Joyce C. Tucker. *Presbyterian Polity for Church Officers.* 3d ed. Louisville: Ky.: Geneva Press, 1999.

Handy Pamphlet for Sessions and Trustees, Synod of New Jersey. Trenton, N.J.: MacCrellish & Quigley, 1913.

Johnson, Earl S. Jr. *The Presbyterian Deacon, An Essential Guide.* Louisville, Ky.: Geneva Press, 2002.

———. *Selected to Serve. A Guide for Church Officers.* Louisville, Ky.: Geneva Press, 2000.

———. *Witness without Parallel, Eight Biblical Texts That Make Us Presbyterian.* Louisville, Ky.: Geneva Press, 2003.

MacInnis, John Murdock. *The Trustee and the Church Today. A Study in the Christian Way of Doing Business.* Philadelphia: Presbyterian Board of Christian Education, 1939.

McLeod, Thomas E. *The Work of the Church Treasurer.* Rev. ed. Valley Forge, Pa.: Judson Press, 1992.

A Manual for Ruling Elders and Church Sessions Containing the Laws and Usages of the Presbyterian Church in the U.S.A. in Relation to Ruling Elders and Other Church Officers, Church Sessions, Churches, and Congregations. Philadelphia: Presbyterian Board of Publication and Sabbath-School Work, 1897, 1912.

The Nature of the Church and the Practice of Governance. Approved by the 205th General Assembly (1993). Louisville, Ky.: Office of the General Assembly, 1993.

Olsen, Charles M. *Transforming Church Boards into Communities of Spiritual Leaders.* Washington, D.C.: Alban Institute, 1995.

Parker, Joel, and T. Balston Smith. *The Presbyterian's Handbook of the Church. For the Use of Members, Deacons, Elders, and Ministers.* New York: Harper & Brothers Publishing, 1861.

Understanding My Trusteeship: For Trustees. Philadelphia: Presbyterian Board of Education, n.d.

Wagner, Hugh. D. *The Relationship of Sessions and Trustees: The Presbyterian Form of Government Considered in Its Bearing on the Control of Ecclesiastical Property; With Particular Regard to State Laws in Relation to Incorporated Ecclesiastical Societies.* Philadelphia: Presbyterian Board of Education, 1906.

Witherspoon, Eugene D., and Marvin Simmers, editors. *Called to Serve: A Workbook for Training Nominating Committees and Church Officers.* Louisville, Ky.:

Curriculum Publishing, Presbyterian Church (U.S.A.), 1994.

Reformed and Presbyterian Background

Calvin, John. *Institutes of the Christian Religion.* Edited by John T. McNeill and translated by Ford Lewis Battles. Philadelphia: Westminster Press, 1960.

———. *Instruction in Faith (1537).* Translated by Paul T. Fuhrmann. Philadelphia: Westminster Press, 1949; Louisville, Ky.: Westminster/John Knox Press, 1992.

A Digest, Compiled from the Records of the Presbyterian Church in the United States of America, And for the Records of the Late Synod of New York and Philadelphia. Philadelphia: Printed for the Trustees of the Assembly by R. P. McCulloh, 1820.

Little, David. "Economic Justice and the Grounds for a Theory of Progressive Taxation in Calvin's Thought." In *Reformed Faith and Ethics,* ed. Robert L. Stivers, 61–84. Lanham, Md., New York, London: University Press of America, 1989.

McKee, Elsie Ann. *Diakonia in the Classical Reformed Tradition and Today.* Grand Rapids: William B. Eerdmans Publishing Co., 1989.

Minutes of the Presbyterian Church in America 1706–1788. Edited by Guy S. Klett. Philadelphia: Presbyterian Historical Society, 1976.

Presbyterian Social Witness Policy Compilation. Louisville, Ky.: Advisory Committee on Social Witness Policy of the General Assembly Council, Presbyterian Church (U.S.A.), 2000.

Selected Theological Statements of the Presbyterian Church (U.S.A.) General Assemblies (1956–1998). Louisville, Ky.: Office of Theology and Worship, Congregational Ministries Division, Presbyterian Church (U.S.A.), 1998.

Stone, Ronald H. "The Reformed Economic Ethics of John Calvin." In *Reformed Faith and Ethics*, ed. Robert L. Stivers, 33–48. Lanham, Md., New York, London: University Press of America, 1989.

Understanding My Trusteeship, For Trustees. Philadelphia: Office of Adult Work, Presbyterian Board of Education, n.d.

Your Church and Your Job, Elders–Deacons–Trustees. Philadelphia: Department of Adult Work, Presbyterian Board of Christian Education, n.d.

The Church as a Corporation

Boush, G. M. *Rulings by the Civil Courts Governing Religious Societies. A Collection of Decisions by State and Federal Courts on the Rights, Powers, and Duties of Religious Societies, Their Members and Judicatories, and Their Property Rights.* Cleveland: Central Publishing House, 1915.

Bradley, Gerard V. *Church-State Relationships in America*. Contributions in Legal Studies, No. 37. New York, Westport, Conn., and London: Greenwood Press, 1987.

Couser, Richard B. *Ministry and the American Legal System. A Guide for Clergy, Lay Workers, and Congregations*. Minneapolis: Fortress Press, 1993.

Davis, Derek H. *Religion and the Continental Congress 1774–1789*. Oxford: Oxford University Press, 2000.

The Legal Resource Manual for Presbyterian Church (U.S.A.) Middle Governing Bodies and Churches 2000–2003. Louisville, Ky.: General Assembly Council Office of Legal/Risk Management Services, 2000. Available on the website: www.pcusa.org.

The Re-Forming Tradition, Presbyterians and Mainstream Protestantism. Edited by Milton J. Coalter, John M. Mulder, and Louis B. Weeks. Louisville, Ky.: Westminster/John Knox Press, 1992.

Weeks, Louis B. "The Incorporation of the Presbyterians." In *The Organizational Revolution, Presbyterians and American Denominationalism*. Edited by Milton J. Coalter, John M. Mulder, and Louis B. Weeks, 37–54. Louisville, Ky.: Westminster/John Knox Press, 1992.

Biblical Models

Adkins, Lesley and Roy A. *Handbook to Life in Ancient Rome*. New York and Oxford: Oxford University Press, 1994.

Beyer, Hermann W. *"kubernēsis."* In *Theological Dictionary of the New Testament*. Edited by Gerhard Kittel. Translated by Geoffrey W. Bromiley. Grand Rapids: William B. Eerdmans Publishing Co., 1965, 3:1035–37.

Conzelmann, Hans. *A Commentary on the First Epistle to the Corinthians*. Hermenia. Philadelphia: Fortress Press, 1975.

Delling, Gerhard. *"Antilambanomai, antilēmpsis, sunantilambanomai."* In *Theological Dictionary of the New Testament*. Edited by Gerhard Kittel. Translated by Geoffrey W. Bromiley. Grand Rapids: William B. Eerdmans Publishing Co., 1964, 1:375–76.

Fee, Gordon D. *The First Epistle to the Corinthians*. New International Commentary on the New Testament. Grand Rapids: William B. Eerdmans Publishing Company, 1987.

Fitzmyer, Joseph A. *Romans, A New Translation with Introduction and Commentary*. Anchor Bible. New York: Doubleday, 1993.

Hays, Richard B. *First Corinthians*. Interpretation, A Bible Commentary for Teaching and Preaching. Louisville, Ky.: John Knox Press, 1997.

Michel, Otto. *"oikonomos, oikonomia."* In *Theological Dictionary of the New Testament*. Edited by Gerhard Kittel. Translated by Geoffrey W. Bromiley. Grand Rapids: William B. Eerdmans Publishing Co., 1967, 5:149–53.

Thiselton, Anthony C. *The First Epistle to the Corinthians, A Commentary on the Greek Text*. Grand Rapids and Cambridge, U.K.: William B. Eerdmans Publishing Co., 2002.

INDEXES

Index of Scriptural References

Index of *Book of Order* References

Index of Subjects